## On Your Plate

# Fruit

## Honor Head

**W**

**FRANKLIN WATTS**

LONDON • SYDNEY

First published in 2007 by Franklin Watts

Franklin Watts
338 Euston Road, London NW1 3BH

Franklin Watts Australia
Level 17/207 Kent St, Sydney, NSW 2000

Copyright © Franklin Watts 2007

Created by Taglines
Design: Sumit Charles; Harleen Mehta, Q2A Media
Picture research: Pritika Ghura, Q2A Media

ISBN: 978 0 7496 7628 5

Dewey classification: 641.3′4

A CIP catalogue for this book is available from the British Library.

Picture credits
t=top b=bottom c=centre l=left r=right m= middle

Cover Images: Shutterstock
Carole Gomez/ Shutterstock: 6tl, Hugo Chang: 6b, Elena Kalistratova/ Shutterstock: 7b, Ljupco Smokovski/ Shutterstock: 8tl, ann
triling/ Shutterstock: 8bl, Olga Lyubkina/ Shutterstock: 8br, Photononstop/ Photolibrary: 9b, Simon Krzic/ Shutterstock: 10, Tina
Rencelj/ Istockphoto: 11bl, Lim Yong Hian/ Shutterstock: 11br, Paul Bodea/ Shutterstock: 12bl, SERDAR YAGCI/ Shutterstock: 12br,
Tomas Bogner/ Shutterstock: 13b, Chris Bence/ Shutterstock: 14l, Yuriy Korchagin/ Shutterstock: 14r, Shanta Giddens/ Shutterstock:
15, Rade Lukovic/ Shutterstock: 16, Gene_l | Dreamstime.com: 17, David Kay/ Shutterstock: 18, Rognar | Dreamstime.com: 19, Tray
Berry/ Istockphoto: 20, Jose Manuel Gelpi Diaz/ Shutterstock: 21.

Printed in China

Franklin Watts is a division of Hachette Children's Books,
an Hachette Livre UK company.

# Contents

# What is fruit?

Fruit is food that grows on plants, such as trees and bushes.

Apples grow on trees.

All fruits have seeds, pips or stones. New plants grow from these.

The middle of the apple is called the core. This is where the pips are.

pip

# Oranges

orange

satsuma

Oranges are a citrus fruit.
They are very good for you.

segment

peel

tangerine

All citrus fruit has a skin called peel.

You eat oranges in pieces called segments. You can also drink orange juice.

Eating oranges and drinking juice helps to stop you from getting a cold.

# Melons

watermelon

Melons are sweet and juicy.
You can eat them sliced.

seeds

gala melon

honeydew

There are lots of different types of melon.

8

All melons have seeds inside.
You must be careful not to
eat the seeds.

Melons are
delicious on a hot
summer's day.

# Pears

Pears grow on trees. They hang down by their brown stalk.

These ripe pears are ready to pick.

Most pears are soft and sweet. Some pears are hard.

pips

Pears have small pips in the middle.

11

# Pineapples

Pineapples have spiky green leaves on the top.

Pineapples are very juicy.

A pineapple has a rough, brown skin. You must cut off the skin before you eat the fruit.

You can cut a pineapple into slices or cubes.

# Bananas

Bananas grow in bunches. When they are growing they are green.

green bananas just picked

ripe bananas

Ripe bananas have bright yellow skin.

14

# To eat a banana, just peel back the skin.

Have a banana for a quick and filling snack.

15

# Peaches

Peaches have a soft, furry skin that you can eat.

stone

 Watch out for the big stone in the middle.

You can buy sliced skinned peaches in a tin. They taste smooth and sweet.

Try tinned peaches with your breakfast cereal.

# Grapes

You can buy grapes in big or small bunches.

 Grapes grow on a plant called a vine.

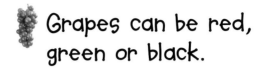 Grapes can be red, green or black.

Some grapes have little pips in the middle. Try not to swallow the pips.

# Strawberries

Strawberries are soft and sweet. They are covered in tiny seeds.

 You can eat all the strawberry, but not the green part.

Strawberries are eaten mostly in the summer.

Strawberries are good to eat on their own, or with cream.

# Things to do

## Which one?

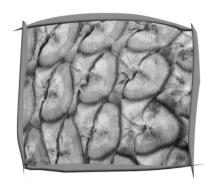 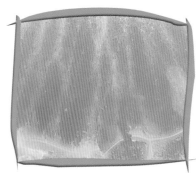 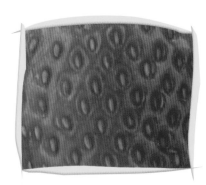

Which of these fruits is a strawberry? Which is an orange? What is the other fruit?

## Guess it!

You can play this game with a friend or in a group. Begin by saying, "My favourite fruit is…". Then you have to say what it looks like and how it tastes. But you must not say its name.

The first person to guess the name of your fruit has the next go.

# Fruit puzzle

How many different fruits can you see in this puzzle?
Can you name them all?

# Glossary

**bushes**
Plants that have lots of branches and leaves which grow out sideways. A bush is usually smaller than a tree.

**citrus fruit**
Fruit, such as oranges and tangerines, that are very juicy and have a skin called peel.

**ripe**
When a food which grows is ready to pick and eat.

**skinned**
Fruit that has had all its skin taken off.

# Index